HOW DID BARNUM BROWN DISCOVER THE WORLD'S MOST FAMOUS DINOSAUR?

DINOSAUR BOOK GRADE 2

CHILDREN'S DINOSAUR BOOKS

Speedy Publishing LLC

40 E. Main St. #1156

Newark, DE 19711

www.speedypublishing.com

Copyright 2017

In this book, we're going to talk about how Barnum Brown discovered the world's most famous dinosaur. So, let's get right to it!

BARNUM BROWN

WHO WAS BARNUM BROWN?

Barnum Brown was the most famous dinosaur bone collector of all time. He was named after P.T. Barnum, the well-known circus showman, because his parents wanted him to do something fantastic with his life. Even though he wasn't related to P.T. Barnum, they did have some things in common.

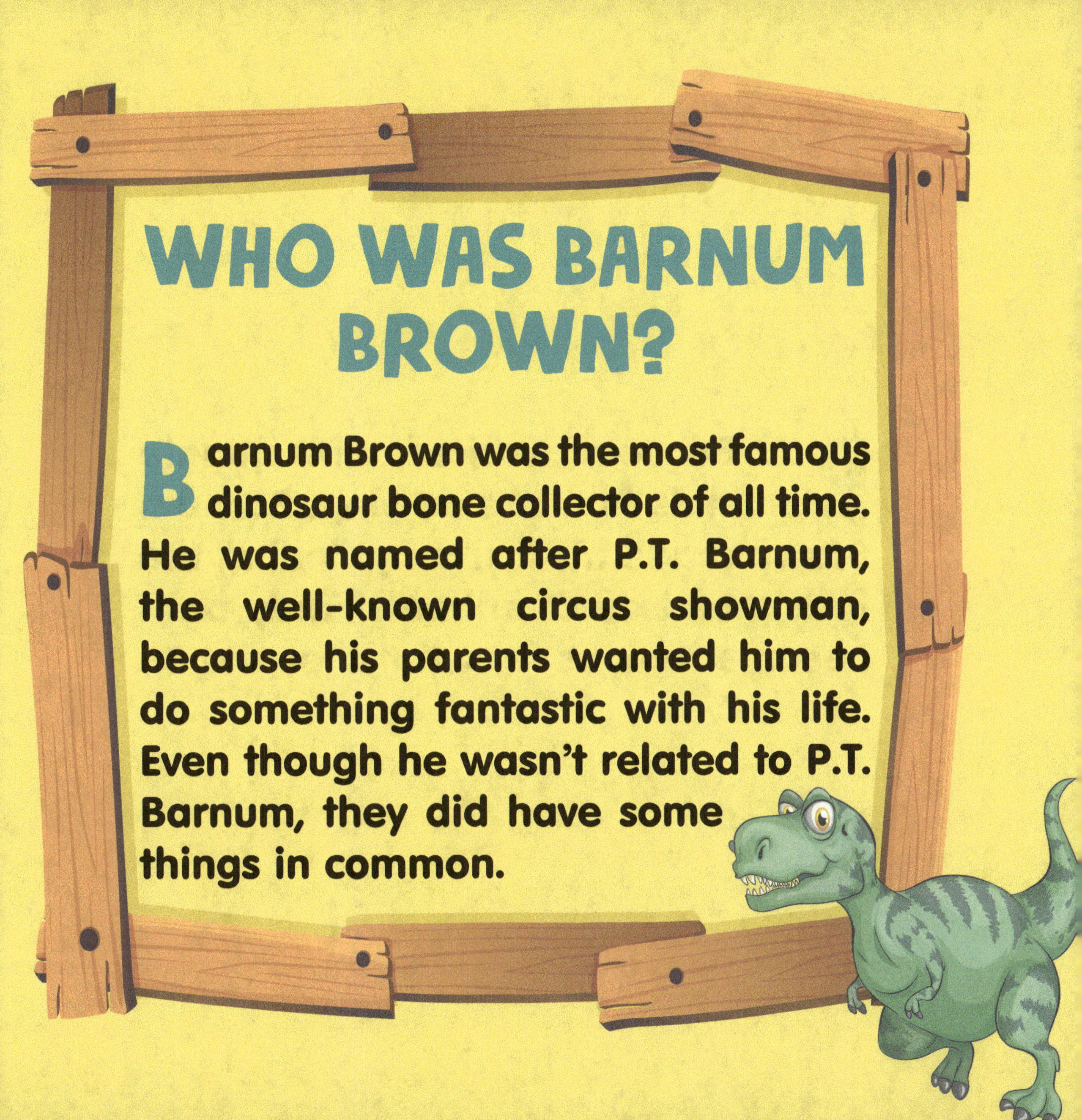

P.T. Barnum worked with jungle animals to make a living. Barnum Brown made his living by finding the fossils of extinct animals. They both became famous for what they did.

PHINEAS T. BARNUM

PALEONTOLOGIST DIG DINOSAUR SKELETON

Barnum became a paleontologist. A paleontologist is a scientist who studies fossils. During his lifetime, Barnum Brown was an adventurer, a fossil hunter, and a spy. He also invented his own techniques for working with fossils.

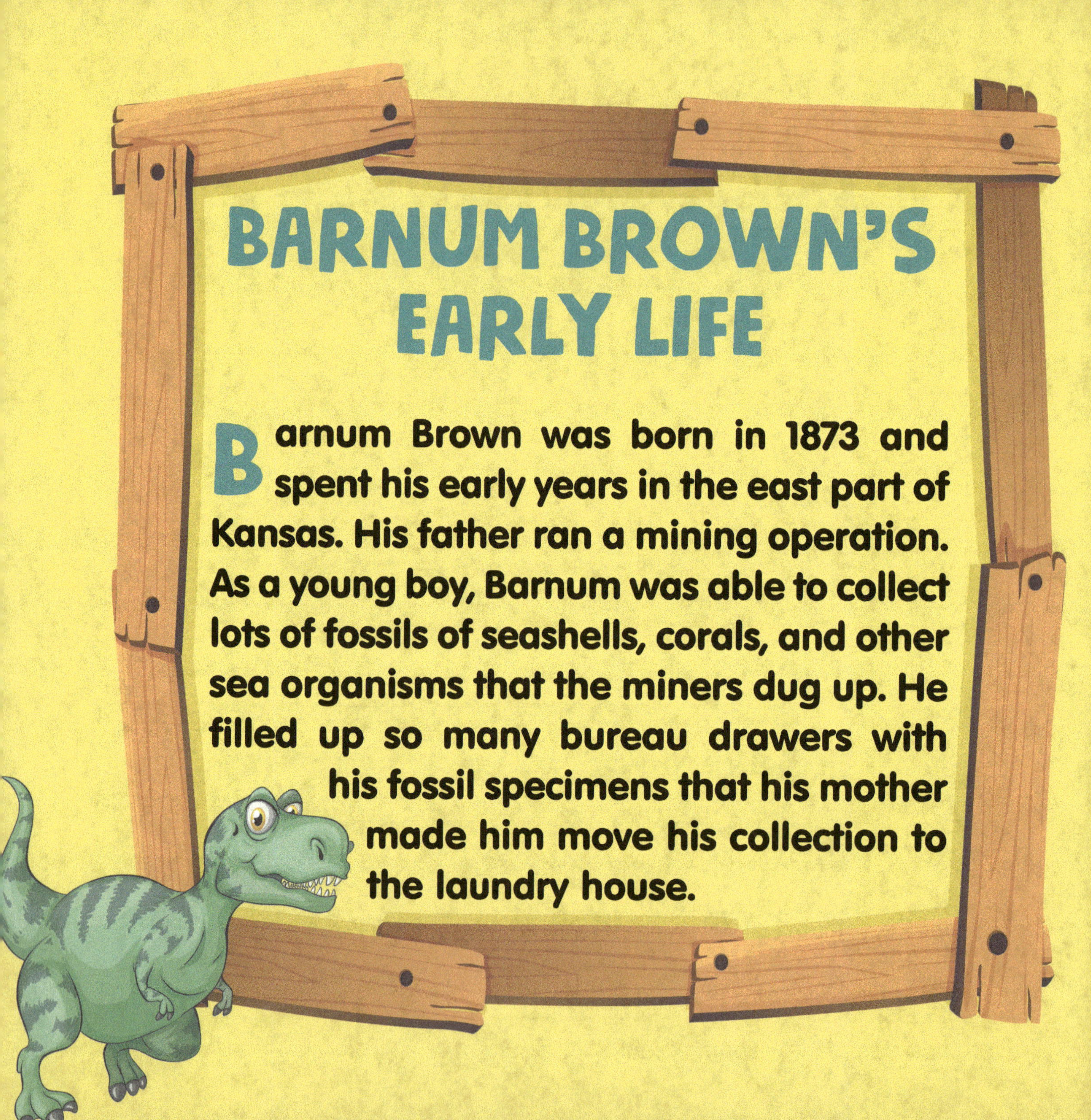

BARNUM BROWN'S EARLY LIFE

Barnum Brown was born in 1873 and spent his early years in the east part of Kansas. His father ran a mining operation. As a young boy, Barnum was able to collect lots of fossils of seashells, corals, and other sea organisms that the miners dug up. He filled up so many bureau drawers with his fossil specimens that his mother made him move his collection to the laundry house.

BADANDS NATIONAL PARK OF SOUTH DAKOTA

COLLEGE YEARS

At the University of Kansas, Barnum studied paleontology and fossil fuels. During the summer, he went on field trips to the badlands in South Dakota and to Wyoming's plains. In 1896, during his summer field trip, he started to work with a field crew from the American Museum of Natural History.

They were hunting for fossils in the San Juan Basin of New Mexico as well as the Bighorn Basin in Wyoming. He showed his excitement and skill at working with fossils so the heads of the museum hired him, even though he hadn't finished his college degree yet.

SCENIC VIEW OVER THE SAN JUAN BASIN BADLANDS

DIPLODOCUS BROWSING A SELECTION OF TREES

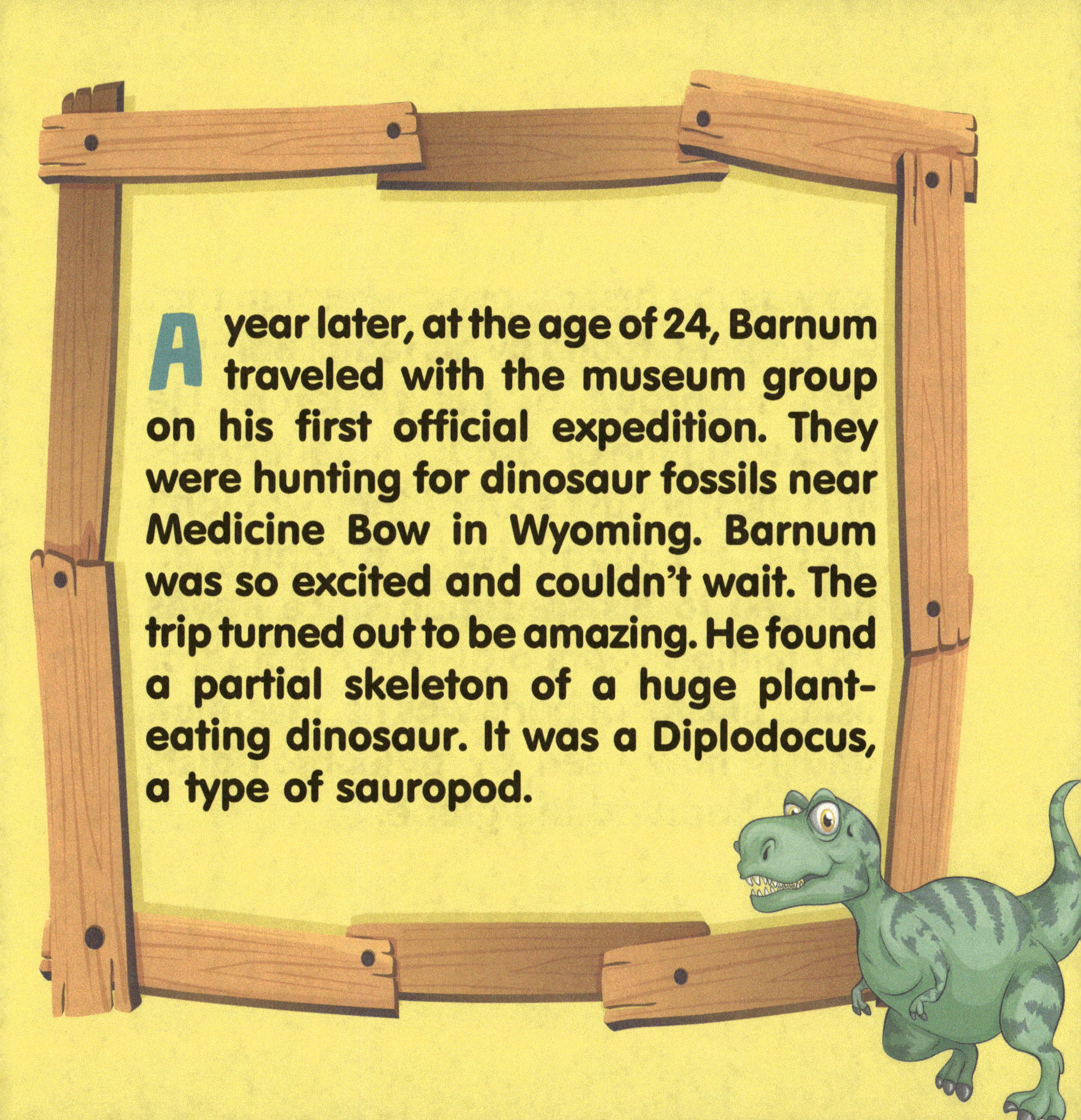

A year later, at the age of 24, Barnum traveled with the museum group on his first official expedition. They were hunting for dinosaur fossils near Medicine Bow in Wyoming. Barnum was so excited and couldn't wait. The trip turned out to be amazing. He found a partial skeleton of a huge plant-eating dinosaur. It was a Diplodocus, a type of sauropod.

It was the first dinosaur skeleton that had been found by his team. Barnum was so proud of his skeleton! He packed up the dinosaur's hindquarters in a plaster cast so that they wouldn't break. He didn't want anything to happen to his specimen since it was 150 million years old! This method of using plaster of paris was his invention and is now used by paleontologists around the globe.

PLASTER OF PARIS

HENRY FAIRFIELD OSBORN

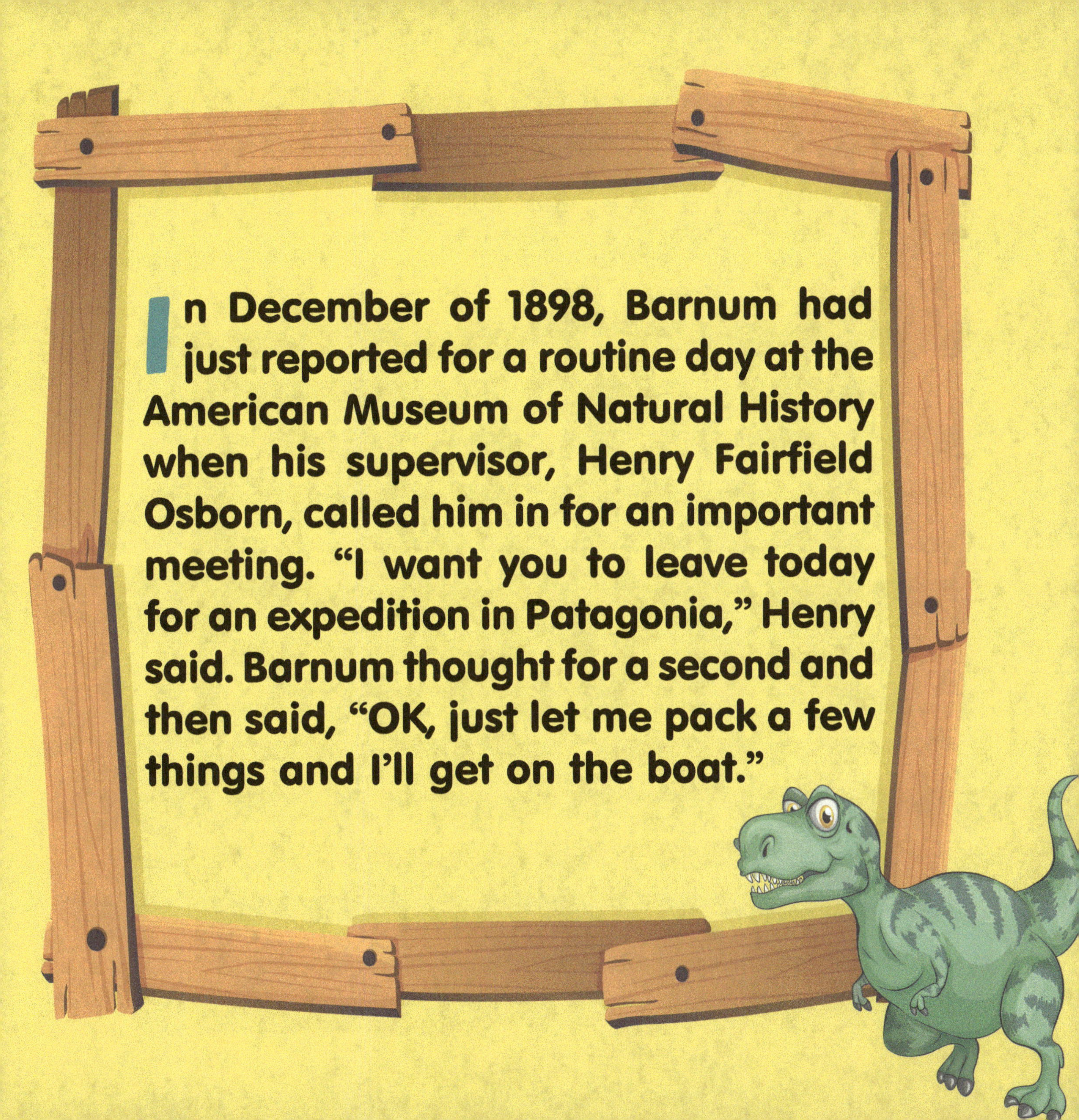

In December of 1898, Barnum had just reported for a routine day at the American Museum of Natural History when his supervisor, Henry Fairfield Osborn, called him in for an important meeting. "I want you to leave today for an expedition in Patagonia," Henry said. Barnum thought for a second and then said, "OK, just let me pack a few things and I'll get on the boat."

Barnum had never been out of the United States before and this was a big adventure! He was going to the southern tip of South America. When he got there, he prospected for fossils by himself. He worked there for over a year. During one trip he was shipwrecked when a huge wave crashed into his boat. He couldn't swim but he grabbed a barrel and hung on tight as he floated to shore. Eventually, he sent over 4 tons of fossil bones of mammals back to the museum.

HELL CREEK

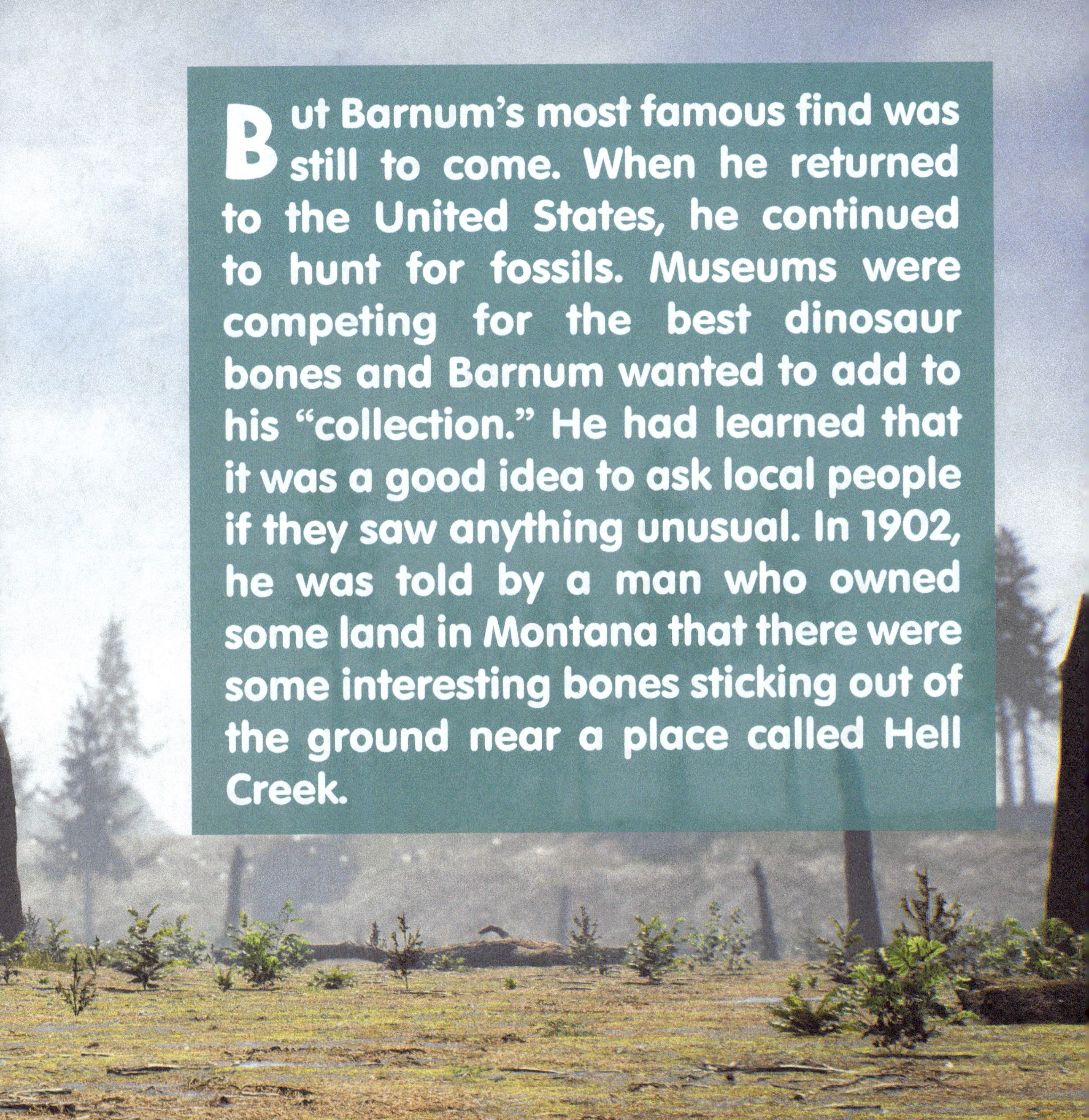

But Barnum's most famous find was still to come. When he returned to the United States, he continued to hunt for fossils. Museums were competing for the best dinosaur bones and Barnum wanted to add to his "collection." He had learned that it was a good idea to ask local people if they saw anything unusual. In 1902, he was told by a man who owned some land in Montana that there were some interesting bones sticking out of the ground near a place called Hell Creek.

When Barnum got there, he was so excited to see that the bones seemed to form a giant skull. It was an enormous dinosaur of the theropod family with huge teeth. This was a fantastic find! However, it was going to take a lot of work to get this extinct beast out from its resting place. It took Barnum and his team three years to get the dinosaur's bones completely out of the ground.

TYRANNOSAURUS REX

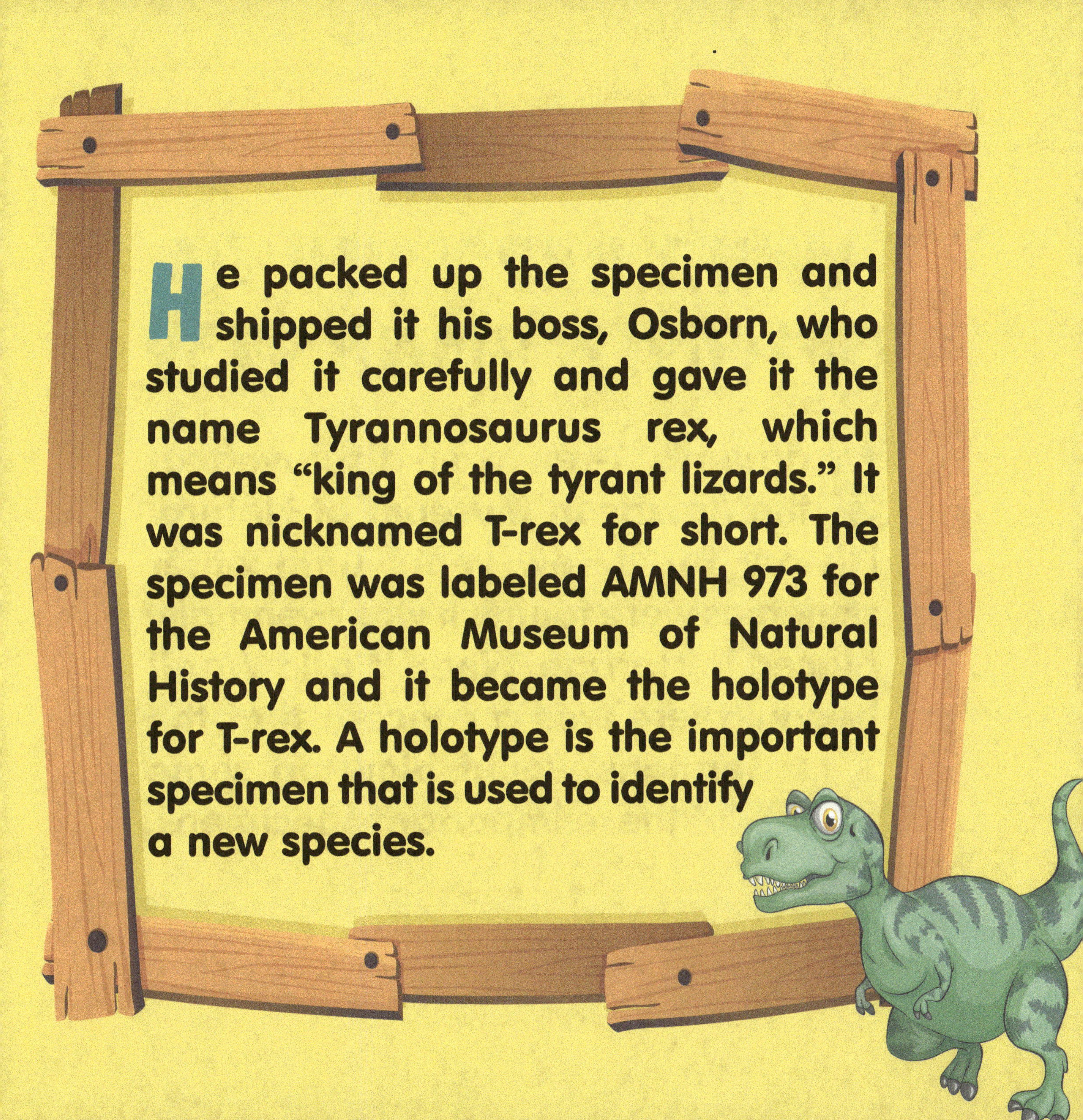

He packed up the specimen and shipped it his boss, Osborn, who studied it carefully and gave it the name Tyrannosaurus rex, which means "king of the tyrant lizards." It was nicknamed T-rex for short. The specimen was labeled AMNH 973 for the American Museum of Natural History and it became the holotype for T-rex. A holotype is the important specimen that is used to identify a new species.

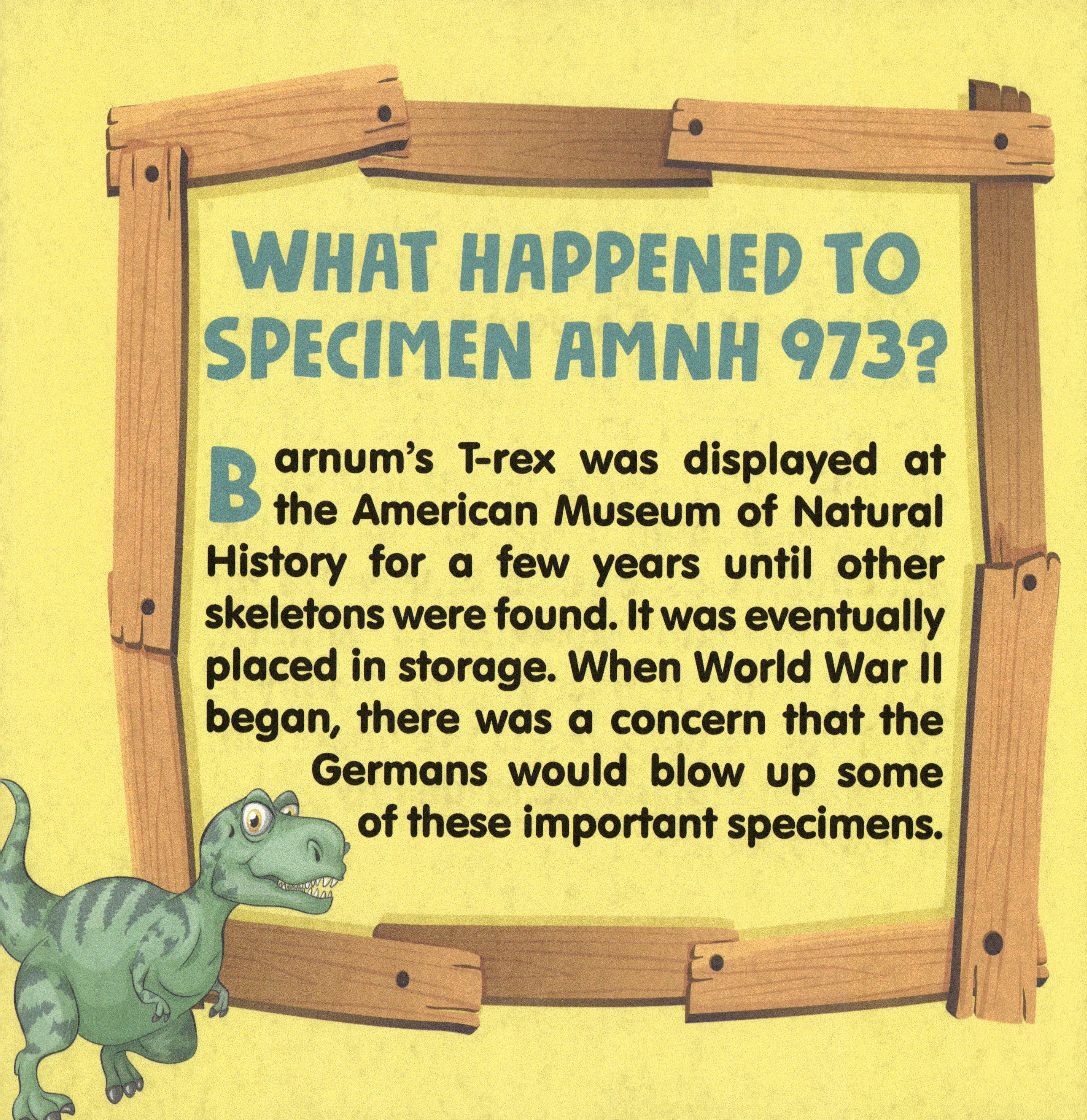

WHAT HAPPENED TO SPECIMEN AMNH 973?

Barnum's T-rex was displayed at the American Museum of Natural History for a few years until other skeletons were found. It was eventually placed in storage. When World War II began, there was a concern that the Germans would blow up some of these important specimens.

AMERICAN MUSEUM OF NATURAL HISTORY

CARNEGIE MUSEUM PITTSBURGH

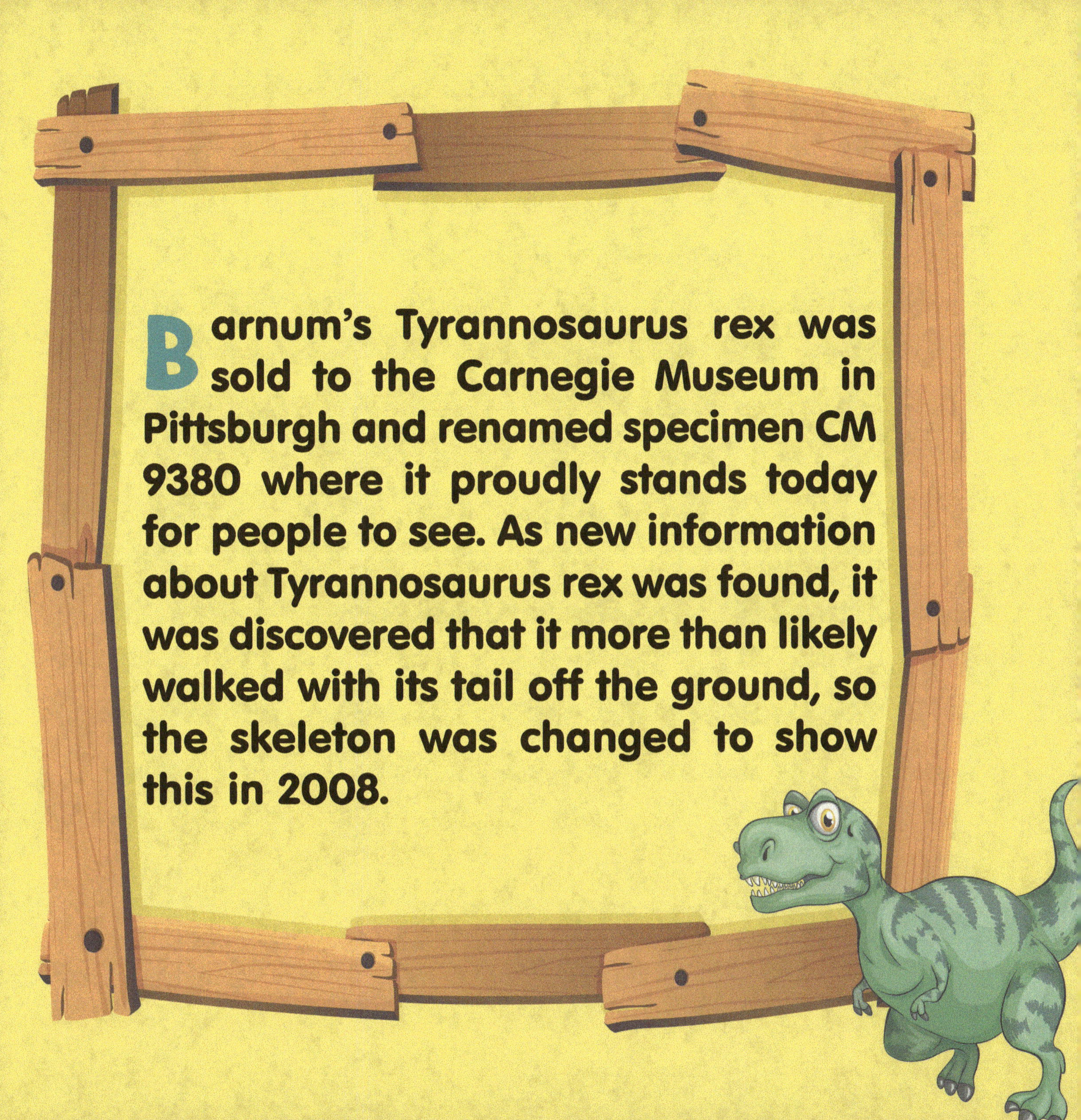

Barnum's Tyrannosaurus rex was sold to the Carnegie Museum in Pittsburgh and renamed specimen CM 9380 where it proudly stands today for people to see. As new information about Tyrannosaurus rex was found, it was discovered that it more than likely walked with its tail off the ground, so the skeleton was changed to show this in 2008.

BARNUM BROWN BECOMES FAMOUS

Barnum was only 29 when he discovered and began to dig up the Tyrannosaurus rex. He became a science celebrity. He was nicknamed "Mr. Bones" as he traveled the American West finding new and unusual fossils wherever he went. On cold days he showed up at the dig site wearing a huge fur coat. He was a larger-than-life person just like the Barnum he had been named after.

SECRET SPY

Droves of people showed up when they found out he was coming to their town. In addition to his adventures digging up dinosaurs, he collected important information for the United States government during both World Wars as he traveled. He was an intelligence agent and spy.

Barnum Brown did field work collecting dinosaur bones for most of his life. He lived for 90 years and gathered so many fossil specimens of different dinosaurs that the museums where they were shipped still have some in boxes.

They don't have enough people to go through all his collections. The American Museum of Natural history has about 80 specimens and over 30 were discovered by Barnum.

Barnum found 5 different specimens of T-rex during his career.

PTEROSAUR DINOSAUR

While he was hunting for fossils, he uncovered information about why the dinosaurs died out 65 million years ago. He also made the connection between dinosaurs and birds. Today, paleontologists are still making discoveries about how birds evolved from dinosaurs.

THE FASCINATING TYRANNOSAURUS REX

Barnum Brown isn't the only person who was fascinated by dinosaurs at an early age. Most people are fascinated by these extinct beasts and many people wonder if someday there will be a real "Jurassic Park" that Steven Spielberg showed in his movie.

KUALOA RANCH - FILM LOCATION OF "JURASSIC PARK"
IN OAHU, HAWAII

PRIMITIVE MAN

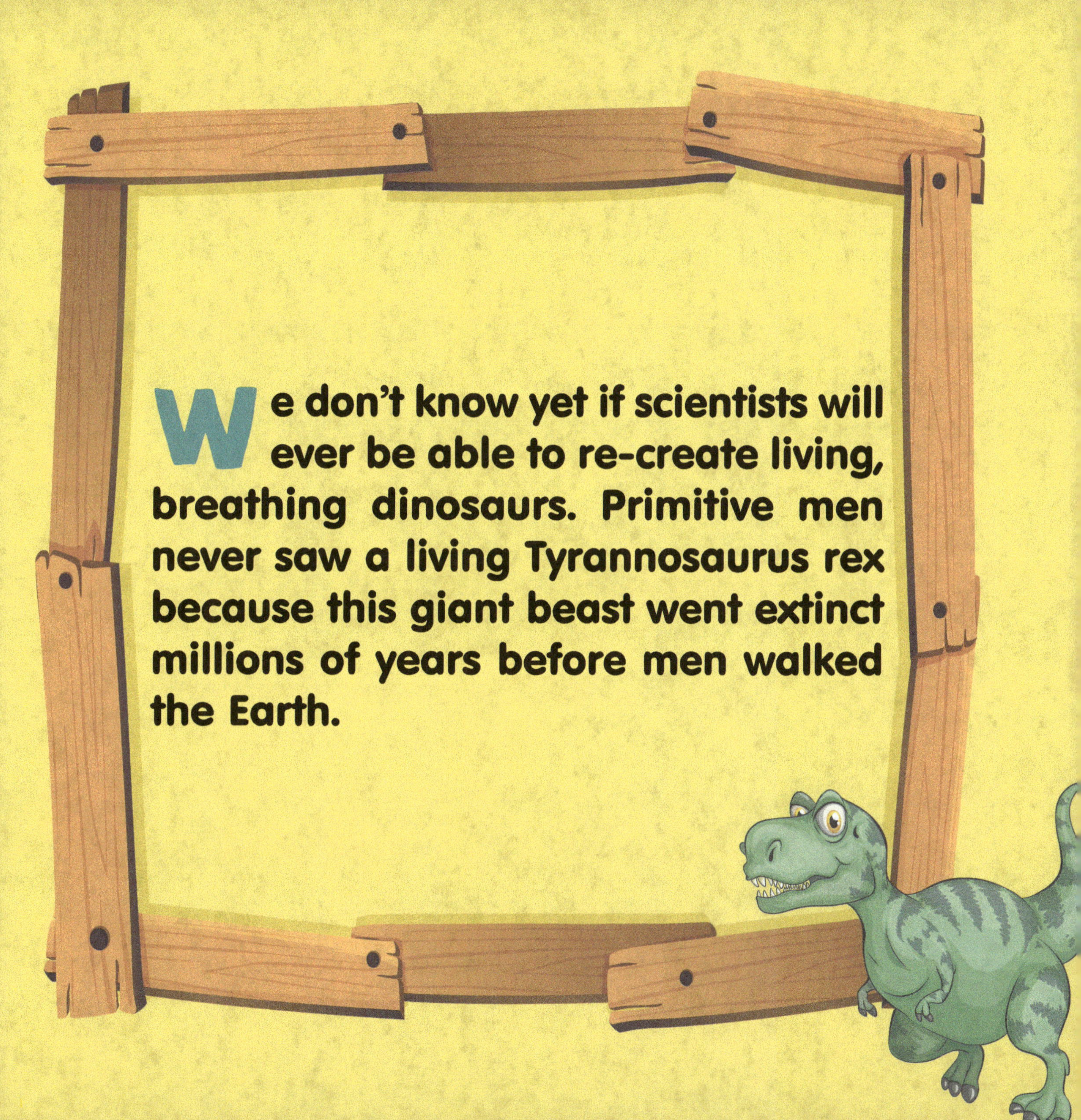

We don't know yet if scientists will ever be able to re-create living, breathing dinosaurs. Primitive men never saw a living Tyrannosaurus rex because this giant beast went extinct millions of years before men walked the Earth.

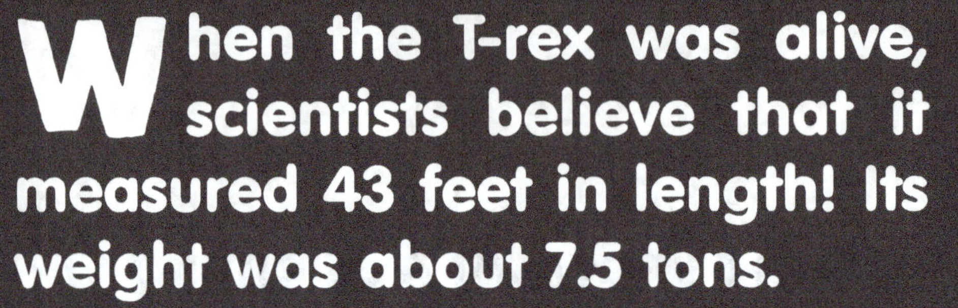

When the T-rex was alive, scientists believe that it measured 43 feet in length! Its weight was about 7.5 tons.

TYRANNOSAURUS REX SKULL

One of the scariest things about the Tyrannosaurus rex was its enormous skull. Some skeletons have been found with skulls that are 5 feet in length.

TYRANNOSAURUS REX TEETH

It had a powerful bite that was so strong it could crush the bones of its prey. It had very sharp, 12-inch long teeth in its jaws.

HOW DID THE T-REX WALK?

T-rex was bipedal, which simply means it walked on its two powerful legs. The legs had to support its massive weight. There is one thing about T-rex that seems wrong for its size. Surprisingly, this huge dinosaur had very tiny arms. Scientists believe that its arms were strong enough to keep a tight grip on its prey.

DINOSAUR FEET WALKING OF TYRANNOSAURUS

A MIGHTY TYRANNOSAURUS REX HUNTS FOR PREY IN A DENSE JUNGLE.

WHAT DID THE TYRANNOSAURUS REX EAT?

Paleontologists know that T-rex ate meat. However, it's not clear whether it hunted down that meat or just scared away other dinosaurs that had already killed the prey so it could eat their leftovers. If it hunted its own food, it was a predator.

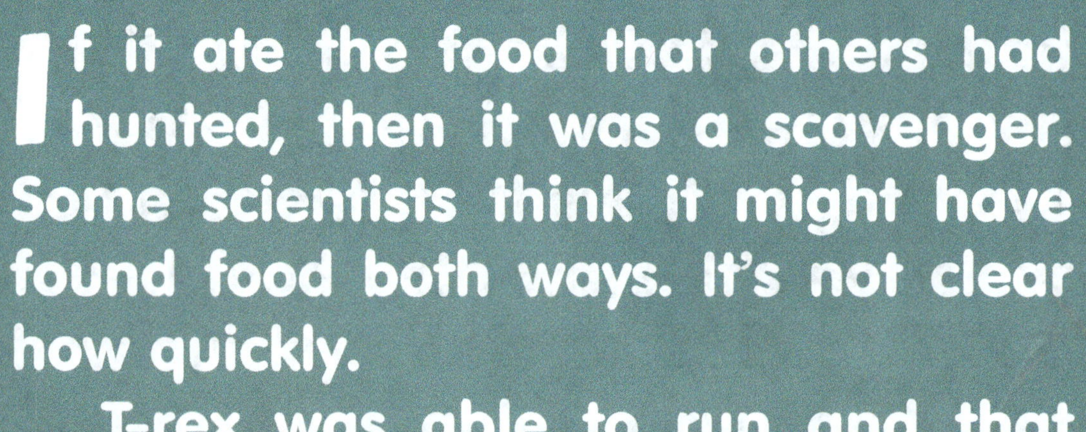

f it ate the food that others had hunted, then it was a scavenger. Some scientists think it might have found food both ways. It's not clear how quickly.

T-rex was able to run and that would make a difference in whether it hunted or not.

Awesome! Now you know more about Barnum Brown and his famous fossil of the dinosaur Tyrannosaurus rex. You can find more Dinosaur books from Baby Professor by searching the website of your favorite book retailer.

Visit

BABY PROFESSOR
EDUCATION KIDS

www.BabyProfessorBooks.com
to download Free Baby Professor eBooks
and view our catalog of new and exciting
Children's Books